PRAISE FOR *BITTER CREEK*

"Like the railroad tracks, two stories exist side-by-side in one incredible piece of work. *Bitter Creek*, told with tension and power, recounts the competition between newly arrived Chinese immigrants and the white men already present in the space between Colorado and Wyoming. In the midst of environmental destruction is the colonialism of the country and the burden of racial hatred, all spoken behind the ethical consciousness of this brilliant writer."

—LINDA HOGAN, *A History of Kindness*

"*Bitter Creek* weaves a polyphony of voices at odds with one another driven by conflicting motivations such as profit, labor, survival, and disputes over space. Set in a harsh and unforgiving time and place, these poems explore a past so brutal that it's tempting to want to forget. However, Goh urges us to remember and honor these voices by keeping their stories alive."

—LISA BICKMORE, Utah poet laureate

"Goh brings to life a cast of historical characters facing challenges so horrific we'd be tempted to call it 'unimaginable' until we see the motivations made plain on the page. Inventive, thought-provoking, and impeccably researched, *Bitter Creek* is as compelling as it is crucial."

—ANA MARIA SPAGNA, *Pushed*

"A striking study of the Rock Springs Massacre, this collection, with poems mined directly from historical documents, is carefully wrought to reckon with the past that still reverberates across our Western mountain passes. Each poem is laced with an empathy that fills in the unspoken and unwritten sides of the story, revealing the timeless truths of greed, blame, and human longing."

—MICHAELA RIDING, The King's English Bookshop

"In this aptly named collection, Goh's narratives give voice to the characters who, without feeling that they have any way out, are caught up in the economic, cultural and racial conflicts culminating in the 1885 Rock Springs Massacre. The refrain, 'The Chinese must go,' echoes throughout these stories, and we hear the pain and confusion within these characters, caught up in an unexpected way of life."

—BARBARA M. SMITH, Wyoming poet laureate

"Goh, acclaimed poet and essayist, blends history and empathic imagination using clear language that creates a compelling story in poetic form. History is not *what*, but *who*, and these pages are filled with the voices of Chinese immigrants, white miners, and industrialists—ordinary people living and working, hoping and struggling. The result is a riveting and complex story of simmering conflict, racism, and finally, the murder of twenty-eight Chinese miners. In bringing to life the Rock Springs Massacre, Goh invites us into a deeper understanding of the past and present of the American West."

—EMILY SINCLAIR, Paonia Books owner

"*Bitter Creek* is nothing short of operatic in the story it unfolds through a sprawling cast of characters and range of lyrical voices. Yet its climactic tragedy is all too real, though nearly erased from American history: the vicious massacre of Chinese mine workers at Rock Springs, Wyoming, in the year 1885. Home, for these poor victims, had shrunk to a place where others 'shared the pain / of living in this strange country alone.' Goh's gift to readers is to restore their forgotten names."

—JULIE KANE, former Louisiana poet laureate

"Goh humanizes the past in this approachable and deeply affecting collection of poems. *Bitter Creek* offers a living history told exquisitely."

—JONATHAN T. BAILEY, *When I Was Red Clay*

BITTER CREEK

Bitter Creek

AN EPIC POEM

Teow Lim Goh

TORREY HOUSE PRESS

Salt Lake City • Torrey

First Torrey House Press Edition, May 2025
Copyright © 2025 by Teow Lim Goh

Published by Torrey House Press
Salt Lake City, Utah
www.torreyhouse.org

International Standard Book Number: 979-8-89092-013-3
E-book ISBN: 979-8-89092-014-0
Library of Congress Control Number: 2024933047

Cover art by Zhi Lin
Cover design by Kathleen Metcalf
Interior design by Gray Buck-Cockayne
Distributed to the trade by Consortium Book Sales and Distribution

Torrey House Press offices in Salt Lake City sit on the homelands of Ute, Goshute,
Shoshone, and Paiute nations. Offices in Torrey are on the homelands of Southern Paiute,
Ute, and Navajo nations.

Contents

IV. A Severe Struggle

V. The Chinese Must Go

Chinese Camp

December 1866
Donner Pass, California

Winter has fallen on us again.
I crawl into my shed in the snow
and curl under my blankets in pain.

All day I shovel as the winds blow.
At night I pray the drifts will not crack
and collapse, carrying me as they mow

down the mountain and breaking my back.
I left a wife and two boys to come
to America, where I lay track,

blast rock, and I try not to succumb
to the ghosts that visit me at night.
Some days I have to make myself numb

and blunt my vision of greater heights.
And I have lost the spirit to fight.

I. Strikebreakers

The Last Spike

May 10, 1869
Promontory, Utah

The restless crowd is smaller than expected.

In the high Sierra, where the mountains still
hold snow, the train that Leland Stanford rode
hit a log that slid onto the tracks and he,
president of the great Central Pacific,
the railroad company that had the vision
to build a line across this steep terrain,
had to wait days before new parts arrived
and workers could repair the damaged cars.

Out in the desert, Stanford had to wait
for three more days under the scorching sky
before the Union Pacific train arrived.

Thomas Durant was on his way out west
when his train halted on the sagebrush steppes
outside Rock Springs, Wyoming, a coal town
a hundred miles from the next railroad stop.
A block of wooden ties lay on the track.
Workers decoupled his dark palace car
and shunted it aside. Four hundred men
held him hostage, demanding their back pay.
"And if you wire for help, we will kill you."
Here in the desert, the vice president
of the great Union Pacific had no choice.
This disobedience he will not forget.

Rain holds them up for two more weary days.
Spring flowers dot the land in red and blue.

At noon they gather where the two lines meet.
Stanford lifts up the sledge and hammers in
the golden spike, his name one of many
engraved onto its side, next to these words:

May God continue
the unity of our country,

as this Railroad unites
the two great Oceans of the world.

He misses, but the telegraph still flashes
DONE from New York to San Francisco, where
the revelries began two days ago,
far from the troubles in these dusty lands.
The distant ranges are still streaked with snow.

The Union Pacific west from Omaha.
The Central Pacific east from Sacramento.

The dream is now fulfilled, the continent tamed.

For two long years the Central Pacific climbed
the deep ravines and rugged granite walls
of the Sierra, working through hot summers
and brutal winters, blasting tunnels in
the stubborn rock, so that it could reach
the summit just to spend a few more months
trying to cross the great Nevada desert,
where for a hundred miles the land is cracked.

Most of the railroad workers were Chinese.
At first the bosses thought these slight young men
could not be strong enough for the hard work
of building in the mountains, a land far
from the warm coastal towns that they call home.
But build the line they did, in record time.

The rails now joined, the trains take turns to pass
over the joint. The engineers on deck
shake hands across the gap and raise a toast
to the good people of America,
who have the fortitude and foresight to build
this feat of muscle and machinery
and ride the rails to its great destiny.

Reporters jostle to take photographs.
A small platoon of soldiers stands at ease.

The officers retreat to their lush cabins,
their private parties. Stanford leaves the scene
at two o' clock, impatient to get back
to more important business.

                                      Out in the sun,
a few Chinese and Irish workmen glance
warily at each other. They lift up
the golden spike—to be returned to Stanford,
now on display in the illustrious college
that bears his name—remove the silver ties,
and drive in the iron for the final strike.

Whiskey Saloon

December 1873
Denver, Colorado

I see them everywhere in hordes,
taking our jobs.

Taking over our country.

Chinamen.
They live like dogs. They even eat dogs.

And what do they do with
their money?

They send it home.

They take and take and never
give back.

The Chinese must go!

Letter Home

December 1873
San Francisco, California

I don't know why it is so difficult.

The railroad was hard work, but it was work.
We knew they paid us less than the white men,
but what could we expect? Debts we must pay.
Our families depend so much on us
to send back money. Now the railroad is done,
and the banks crashed four months ago, I swear
there is no work. I don't know what to do.

Remember my old friend Ah Lum and all
the gold that he brought back from California,
the yellow silks he gave to his new wife,
the large brick home he built for his family?
Look at how well they eat, meat every day.
These days he hardly needs to work at all.

I want to build a paradise for us too.

The railroad life is for young men. I thought
I could save up and go home, but there is never
enough. And I am not young anymore.

Dearest, I don't know what I'm doing wrong.

Number One

March 1874
New York, New York

To write about the New York Stock Exchange
is to simply describe the movements of Jay Gould.
Before he came to the Union Pacific,

he issued fraudulent stock to wrestle the Erie Railroad
away from Cornelius Vanderbilt and drove up
the price of gold until it crashed on Black Friday.

All in a day's work before he goes home
to his family, their faces bright in the portrait
on the mantelpiece. He retires to his own library

but the day still weighs on him, that latest acquisition—
he runs his finger down the ledger of coal mines
in the West. The price of coal is falling,

the price of mining must fall too. He pauses on
Rock Springs, Mine Number One,
the most productive of them all, mouthing

these words under his breath: Mine. Number One.

Landlocked

November 1874
Rock Springs, Wyoming

He returns to air, dusts the soot
off his skin, walks home on the banks

of Bitter Creek, so named for the water
too hard to drink. The stars

a blanket in the sky, telling stories
he cannot yet read. All day he crouches

in a sweltering room, picking at seams
for nuggets of coal, setting charges

to clear the debris. Coal dust
gathers in his lungs. All day he swallows

his tears. All day he tries
not to think of the past. He prays

his lamp keeps flickering
and the old canary keeps singing.

Town Hall

First they cut our wages.

We agreed only if they lowered their prices
at the store.

Now they break their promise.

How will we feed our children if
we keep working for less?

Why do we pay
while they live in their gilt?

I say we call a strike on November 8th.

Restore our pay to five cents a bushel.

November 2nd we start working
half days.

We will not dig extra this winter.

Let's see how far they get
without us.

Let's go for broke.

Housekeeping

November 1875
Rock Springs, Wyoming

No matter how much she scrubs the floor,
the dust returns, a fine silver
on every surface in the house.
"We live in a dugout, dear. It's pointless,"
John tells her, but she cannot
stop—it is not proper
for a woman to live in such a mess.

These days he hardly comes home
for dinner, staying out late
in the union hall—and she knows—
stopping by the saloon for a pint or five
after talking all day about how much longer
to strike. There are only so many ways
she can make their pantry last.

She counts how much she owes the store,
how much for flour, for eggs, maybe
some roast for Sunday—no, that was only
a girlhood dream, like the dream
that he would put his hands on her breasts,
two fingers missing.

Ultimatum

November 5, 1875
Rock Springs, Wyoming

S. H. H. Clark, the general superintendent
of the Union Pacific Coal Department

Does your union propose to dictate to this company
regarding the amount of coal it is to mine?

Do you intend to limit our supply of coal
from our own mines?

Do you wish to cripple us in failing to give us
an adequate supply of coal

for the purpose of running our trains and supplying
the needs of the people
residing along the line of our road?

If that is your purpose, gentlemen,
I herewith give you notice that in a very short time
I will have a body of men here

who will dig for us all the coal we want.

Letter Home

November 19, 1875
San Francisco, California

My dearest wife,

                    I have good news for you.
Yesterday I was praying at the temple
and this big man walked in, saying he needed
a hundred men for a job. I said I built
the railroad, I didn't mind the winter nights,
and I knew how to handle the explosives.
"Great! You're just what we're looking for," he said,
giving me a train pass and telling me
I must be at the depot in the morning.

I'm sorry that I haven't written much
these days. It's hard to stand all day in lines,
waiting for someone, anyone, to call me.
Some nights I think about those years I spent
shoveling snow and blasting rock. I kept
praying a shard won't shatter in my heart.
But I had work. I made money. I know
it's hard for you too. Our dear boys are growing
so fast. And Mother needs her medicines.

I carry your sweet letters in my pocket,
read them again when I long to hear your voice.
I thought I would go home after two years
in California, land of golden peaks
and dreams made on the backs of desperate fools.
No matter how much I work, it never seems
to be enough. I can't say what Wyoming

will bring. I'll still be blasting rock, this time
in the coal mines. I promise to write more

when I get there—

Your faithful husband.

Strikebreakers

November 21, 1875
Rock Springs, Wyoming

Snow falls the night before.
Winds whip the sagebrush, the rocky hills.

Men huddle in their hovels, light the last
oil in their lamps, eat the scraps
left on their stoves.

No work, nowhere to go,
some of them drink all day in the saloons.

Cold seeps under their skins.
Fourteen days—how long more can they hold out?

*

Soldiers arrive in the cover of night,
the moon and stars still shrouded in clouds.

The troops stand guard before the mines, the shops,
the company store, the banks of Bitter Creek,
now a trickle in the dour of winter.

Their footsteps sink into the snow.

They signed up to fight for their country,
for life, liberty, and happiness—

*

Governor Thayer rides the two o'clock
train from Cheyenne.

They dine him in first class,
befitting, they say, a dignitary of the Territory.

The blood of steaks
soaks the mash on their plates.

Wine stains the tablecloth.

They shake hands, whisper plans, and step out
under the cold blue sky—

refusing to look at the men on strike.

*

Four fifteen.

A train pulls up from Sacramento,
its shadow cast across this fractured land.

A hundred and fifty Chinamen alight
still in a daze, their long hair
braided into queues.

They set up camp across the creek, make
dinners of noodles, slicing the pork so thin
the fat glistens in the broth.

That night they sleep in boxcars, wrapped in wool.

*

The strikers plead, "We'll go back to work
if you send those people away."

But the Chinese are here to stay.

The governor says,

>   "Legitimate labor should not
> be interfered with, no matter the race
> and nationality of the laborer.

Law and order will be enforced even
if it takes the might of the army."

The soldiers hide their scowls.

*

Mine Number Three.

Carpenters build huts all morning,
a makeshift Chinatown on the icy ground.

And this, posted at the company store:

> *All persons whose names appear below can obtain*
> *employment at Mine Number One.*
> *None others need apply.*

> *All miners desiring passes*
> *for themselves and their families must apply at once,*
> *as none will be granted after November 24th.*

Those who stay sign their right to strike away.

*

Where else can the white men go?

Rock Springs is a desert
surrounded by mountains and snow,

dependent on the Union Pacific
for work and housing, to get to Omaha or Denver,
Salt Lake City or San Francisco.

Stomping on the muddy ground,

they board the trains to futures unknown,
biting their lips so hard they bleed.

Letter Home

December 1875
Rock Springs, Wyoming

It's a strange place out here. Not snowy
like the mountains
or stormy like the sea.

It's a desert of broken rock.

And it is cold.
We live in wooden huts.
Winds seep through the cracks.

The white men are hostile.

I don't know what happened, but soldiers
escorted us when we arrived.
Company guards protect us in the mines.

But I'm getting paid, finally.
Here's my first paycheck, as I promised.
I don't think I can stay here long, but the money is good.

I want to see you all again.

II. Roads to Exclusion

Faraway Places

September 1880
Rock Springs, Wyoming

Go West, young man, they said
and off he went, dreaming

of mountains and rivers
of gold. Now he has nothing

to his name, no way out
of this town of coal. Whiskey

burns his throat, drowning
the ache of his abode.

Winds shake the windows
and keep him awake as he longs

for a woman's warm breath
to lull him back to sleep.

Expectant

September 1880
Rock Springs, Wyoming

All day she dusts and still she finds
black streaks when she sets down the laundry.
Her feet swell and her back hurts.
Six months along: the baby kicks again.

A stew is bubbling on the stove.
Potatoes, herbs, a little bit of meat.
She drops a plate and looks at the clock.
He should be home by now: an accident
at the mine or one more rowdy round
with the old boys at the bar?
The shards glint in the fading light.

She watches coal crackle on the stove
and dreams of this child she will soon hold,
an angel with Daddy's green eyes
and her chestnut hair—must be a girl,
she knows, she knows, he will come home for her.

She waits to hear his ragged cough outside.

Afternoon Break

September 1880
Rock Springs, Wyoming

This life is not what she wanted.

"It's a promotion," he told her,
"A management position."
But what kind of advancement is this
when they have to live in a town
with more gun shops and saloons
than schools? Why have the nicest
house on the street, when there
is nothing to do and no one
to talk to? She has to send for dresses
from Denver and Cheyenne.

And the people here, a bunch
of hooligans who don't want to work,
who have no sense of right
and wrong, who must be threatened
to get them to do anything.
Worse, the hordes of dirty foreigners—
you just don't know who they are
and what they are thinking. She feels
she is living inside a siege.

She storms onto the porch and grabs
the girl by her arm. "Listen,
you're still too young to know,
the world outside is not like home,
it is not safe, not safe
for pretty girls like you. When those
rough men and their dirty yellow hands

walk past our house, you mustn't
let them see you. Stop playing
in the yard and come inside.
You don't know what men like that
will do to girls like you."

Grievances

September 1880
Rock Springs, Wyoming

Our wages have dropped in the last five years.

They cheat us with false weights.

They make us buy from the company store.

We lay track for no pay.

They hire Chinese while we go without work.

They make us work where the Chinese would not.

They sell tools to the Chinese at cost.

We pay the full price.

They let the Chinese bribe them for the best rooms.

When the Chinese taunt us, they take their side in a fight.

The streets are no longer safe for our women.

They refuse to listen to us.

We cannot strike.

The Chinese must go!

Letter Home

September 1880
Rock Springs, Wyoming

Mother is gone. I read your letter again.
You said she asked for me before she died.
I don't know what to say. Why couldn't I
make it back to see her one more time? I wish
I could have been there to help bury her
and make the offerings I've failed to do
in all these years. I want to hold her hand
again and let her know I love her, she
who gave me life, who gave her only son
the meat while she ate rice and greens without
a word of complaint. I didn't have the money
to cross the ocean twice. And I still don't.
I know it's no excuse, but I keep working,
and yet there never seems to be enough.

Headlines

October 1880
Denver, Colorado

From the Rocky Mountain News

Celestials Corralled.

The Police Make a Raid on the Opium Joints

And Arrest a Number of Chinamen.

Revolting Scenes In and Around Chinatown.

*

The Opium Case.

Coroner's Inquest on the Late W. McClellan,

Which Shows that He Died From Opium Smoking.

Some Startling Revelations About the Horrible Habit.

*

John Chinaman.

The Pest of the Pacific Coast.

The Heathen Who Have Ruined California

And Are Now Slowly Invading Colorado.

Workmen Starving and Women Following Prostitution

Through the Competition of the Wily Heathen.

*

Heathen Hordes.

The Opium Dens are Still in Full Blast,

The Chinese Still Crowding Into the State

Ruining Labor and Encouraging Immorality.

*

The Labor Issue.

Startling Facts on the Cheap Chinese Trade.

The Movement Approved by Prominent Republicans.

A Striking Leaf from General Garfield's Record.

How the Chinese Problem is Regarded on the Coast.

*

Caucasians Against Mongolians—The Survival of the Fittest.

Hop Alley Riot

October 31, 1880
Denver, Colorado

The *Rocky Mountain News*: A white man meets
the Chinese man who does his laundry. Either
he did not pay, or could not pay, or they
could not agree on what he should have paid
for the last wash and now in the saloon
on a Sunday afternoon they start to argue.
Over these ten cents, the Chinese man
takes out a knife and cuts the white man's cheek.
The white man staggers onto Wazee Street,
his bloody face to the assembling crowd.
The Chinese man pulls out a gun and shoots.

As told by saloon keeper John Asmussen:
"There were two quiet Chinese playing pool
when three or four white men stumbled in drunk
and taunted them. So one of the Chinese
asked them to stop. It made them angrier—
they said they were as good as Chinamen
and stormed toward my bar for beer. I served
the beer and as they drank, I gently told
the two Chinese it's better that they leave.
They nodded and snuck out by the back door.
But one of the white men followed them out
with a cue stick and struck a Chinese man,
one of those two, right on his head. His friend
yelled back inside, 'Come on Charley! He's got him!'"
The Chinese tried to get away. Some say
the other Chinese man took out a gun
and fired at the white men, missing each shot.

No matter how it happened, this we know:
A rumor goes about town that a white man
was shot and killed by a rowdy Chinaman.

A mob begins to gather on the streets.
They break into the laundries, opium dens,
brothels, and gambling halls, dragging Chinese
outside to beat them up. The mayor orders
the crowd to scatter and when no one listens,
he tells the firemen to turn on the hoses. Drenched
and furious, the mob torches Chinatown.

Uptown, they clinch a noose around the neck
of a Chinaman and hang him to a post,
leaving his corpse there as a battle cry.

Jim Moon, gambler, desperado, known as
the meanest man in Colorado, stands
before a laundry, gun cocked in each hand.
"This Chinaman does my washing and by God
you will not hurt him!"

                    Madam Lizzie Preston
hides some Chinese in her salon, her girls
armed against the mob with champagne bottles
and high heels.

                    A Chinese man is dragged
along the streets with a rope around his neck.
The rope is cut.

                    Saloons are ordered closed.

The police chief, appointed just this day,
arrives at nightfall with five hundred men,
making arrests and breaking up the mob.
They hold about a hundred Chinese in a jail

on Colfax, kept away from the fury
of the dripping hordes. The rioters they put
in a city jail. All but the four white men
who hung the Chinaman are soon released.

Monday the city remains closed for cleanup.

Election Day's on Tuesday. It is quiet.

Four men are charged with murder, but the courts
acquit them on the grounds that if the city
and county had responded properly,
the mob would not have risen like it did.

In mining camps across the Rocky Mountains,
not one Chinese can be seen anywhere. The mob
may have been quelled, but still these chants are heard:

"Stamp out the yellow plague!"

                    "The Chinese must go!"

Reverse, Reverse

November 1880
San Francisco, California

As governor of California, Leland Stanford said
to his legislature, "To my mind it is clear
that the settlement among us of an inferior race

is to be discouraged by every legitimate means. Asia,
with her numberless millions, sends to our shores
the dregs of her population."

            Later, as the Central Pacific
began its climb to the heights of the Sierra, he needed
the Chinese, those small men who could lift trestles

and chisel rock, who did not strike and worked hard
without complaint.

            Now the violence spreads:
Los Angeles. San Francisco. Denver.

Riots in Chinatown, the streets no longer safe
for the good men and women of the superior race.

And so it must be, the Chinese must go.

Chinese Exclusion Act

May 6, 1882
Washington, District of Columbia

Whereas, in the opinion of the Government of the United States the coming of Chinese laborers to this country endangers the good order of certain localities within the territory thereof:

Therefore,

Be it enacted by the Senate and House of Representatives of the United States of America in Congress assembled,

That from and after the expiration of ninety days next after the passage of this act, and until the expiration of ten years next after the passage of this act, the coming of Chinese laborers to the United States be, and the same is hereby, suspended; and during such suspension it shall not be lawful for any Chinese laborer to come, or having so come after the expiration of said ninety days, to remain within the United States.

...

That hereafter no State court or court of the United States shall admit Chinese citizenship; and all laws in conflict with this act are hereby repealed.

That the words "Chinese laborers," wherever used in this act, shall be construed to mean both skilled and unskilled laborers and Chinese employed in mining.

Letter Home

May 1882
Rock Springs, Wyoming

And it has come to pass. Exclusion's now
the law of this cursed land. At night I gaze

at the full moon and wonder when we can
share a pillow again. I thought that now

Mother is gone, you and the boys can join me
out here. But this barbaric law is aimed

at men like me. Laborers. Coolies. Slaves.
That's what they call us. Only diplomats

and merchants can bring in their families—
if Father hadn't died, if bandits hadn't

ambushed the countryside, I would still be
beside you. And I might have finished school

and become a scholar. But it is useless
to dwell on the past. This is my lot now.

China Mary

March 1883
Evanston, Wyoming

I.

Last night I saw the men who died at Almy
knock on my door and ask for food and water,
their bloodshot eyes darting around my shack.

Some even asked if they could spend the night
with me, relive the good old days. I laughed
and said, "But I am an old woman now,

haggard and wrinkled, no longer the beauty
who you once knew." They tried to sidle up
to me and I woke up all drenched in sweat,

and I remembered it has been two years
since the explosion at the mine, the blast
so strong that we could feel it in Evanston.

Their bodies are still buried in the rubble,
too dangerous to reach. Their spirits still roam
this desert, lost, unable to go home.

II.

It is easy to lose track of time
in these crazy wild desert steppes—
I arrived here fourteen years ago
when the railroad first came to town,
hoping to rebuild my life after
my husband died in a blast.
The white folks think I don't know
a lot of English but I read
their papers every day, and like them
I suppose I came out here
for second chances. I had to go back
to my old profession—it was all
I knew to do, but at least
I didn't need a madame or man.
My money is my own and I could go
as I pleased. In the beginning
the white folks mostly ignored me
but as Chinatown grew here
and in Rock Springs, I learned to make
myself invisible in plain sight.
I am no longer young but the men
are still lonely, longing for the comforts
that remind them of home, the wives
and children they left behind,
heard from only in letters that can take
months to arrive. Sometimes
all they want is someone to listen
over too much opium and wine.

III.

I hardly ever see her leave her house, but when she does
she is always with her servant girl, struggling to walk

with her small feet and her delicate face made up
as if she has somewhere better to go. Her eyes betray

her disappointment: this town is not what she imagined
America would be when she married a merchant

her family must have chosen for her. Lady, this town
is not what any of us had imagined for ourselves

if you had asked us thirty years ago. I hear her yell
at the servant girl over—I don't know what anymore,

nothing is good enough for her. I try to greet her
but she always looks straight past me,

a fallen woman not even worthy of contempt, but Lady,
no one here cares that your husband buys you

silk dresses and sandalwood fans. You are still a
Heathen Chinee, a shiny specimen of a despicable race.

III. Knights of Labor

Night Shift

December 1883
Denver, Colorado

*Joseph Buchanan, a founder
and editor of* The Labor Enquirer

Winds blister the night.

The baby cries, his wife
cradles it.

By candlelight,
he sets type

for the columns he writes.
No one pays

enough for him
to keep on the lights.

But still he writes into the night.

Iron Horse

February 1884
Rock Springs, Wyoming

The winter sun blurs her eyes
as she steps out of the company store.
Once again, the keeper told her
she could have all the eggs and butter
she wanted, even some ham,
some spices from faraway places
she would never get to see—
he'll take it out of next week's paycheck.

She walks home along the creek,
watching a train pull into town, smoke
puffing, wheels screeching,
steel glinting in the midday sun. Up close,
she feels the heat of the engine,
smells the coal burning, as if

its weight is on her body, a machine
that would crush her and keep on flying.

Red Ink

For weeks Jay Gould watched the stock price
of the Union Pacific plummet
on the news

that Congress wants to garnish
more than half its revenues and ordered
an investigation
into the unauthorized distributions of dividends.

It isn't right for the government to put obstacles
in the way of commerce,

his genius,

insisting the company pay back the loan it took
from the Treasury to build
the original road.

Principal: $27,235,512   Interest: 6%   Term: 30 years

As the repayment provisions were badly written,
for a decade
Gould stalled and argued in court
the road was completed

in 1874, not 1869—
all the repairs they had to make—

and he questioned the definition of net earnings.

It is his right to get the highest returns
for his shareholders, but now

the Union Pacific has no more cash to stay afloat.

Wildcat Strike

May 1884
Denver, Colorado

Monday morning
the men arrive at the shop, only

to see on the door:

> NOTICE OF WAGE REDUCTION
> EFFECTIVE IMMEDIATELY

Some get docked ten percent, some twenty-five.

"Why must we put up with this?"

They have no union, but
one by one they walk off the job.

At the end of the day,
all the shopmen of the Union Pacific

from Omaha to Ogden
are on strike.

Letter Home

May 1884
Rock Springs, Wyoming

I don't know why I'm so unlucky.
Did I do something wrong
in a past life and now I have
to pay for it? I've done the things
I was supposed to do and yet
I'm trapped in this rotten place
with no way out. The days
are getting longer and the prairie
is starting to bloom again,
the tiny desert flowers yellow
and red along the creek,
but I hardly see the sun anymore.

The company slashed wages again
and all the shopmen walked out.
I don't quite know what happened
but they organized in Denver
and forced the company to rescind
the cuts. This excited the whites
here in Rock Springs. They asked us
again to join them in demanding
higher wages. We refused.
They spat at us and called us rats.

Who are the rats here? These people
are behind the exclusion laws.
Do they believe we are that stupid?
We took on the Central Pacific
that brutal summer they needed us
to finish the line at all costs.

We don't need them to organize.
They like to talk about solidarity
but we know if anything goes wrong,
we'll be the first to pay the price.

Ousted

Mr. Gould,

Under your leadership in the last ten years, the company
did not pay a single cent of the loans it took out
from the Treasury. All this while you authorized the distribution
of dividends to your shareholders. All this while

you argued the company is a corporation
for the public interest. Now the Treasury wants to garnish
fifty-five percent of our revenues. Our stocks sell
for merely a fraction of their price a week ago.

Mr. Gould, we want you to step down as the director
of the Union Pacific. You will still keep your ownership stake
in the company, but Sidney Dillon will be removed
from his role as president. In his place we will appoint the man

who has shown the most courage in this crisis. Gentlemen,
it is our honor to introduce to you the new president
of the Union Pacific Railway, our good man from Boston:

Charles Francis Adams Jr.

The Agitator

August 1884
Denver, Colorado

Joseph Buchanan came to Colorado
during the Leadville boom,

worked as a printer in this town
where peaks scrape the sky and the earth

yields lodes of silver. But the railroad
came, carrying hordes of men

looking for work. The mines
cut wages and the miners

walked out. For joining their march,
he was fired and run out of town.

Back in Denver, he founded
The Labor Enquirer.

Instead of the price of silver
he quoted the price of dynamite.

In May the shopmen of the Union Pacific
walked out without a union

and asked him to organize them.
"We read your paper."

In four days, the company yielded
to all of his demands.

Now the company cut wages in Kansas
and fired twenty of the men

who led the strike in May. He gave
the orders to walk out today.

Negotiation

August 1884
Omaha, Nebraska

Joseph Buchanan meets with S. H. H. Clark
at the Union Pacific headquarters.

Listen up, boss.

Our demands are reasonable.

One, restore our wages.

Two, reinstate the shopmen you fired.

Three, let all strikers return to work.

Without prejudice.

Four, end the ironclad and let us strike.

This is not for you to decide?

Your new man Adams forced our hand.

Ask him.

He won't hire the men in Denver?

No way.

Now he'll hire all but five?

An injury to one is an injury to all.

Remember what happened in May.

He'll hire all but the secretary of our committee?

Then nothing but passenger trains will run tomorrow.

It takes more than train crews to get trains over the road.

Reinstate him first.

You can investigate later.

Thank you, sir.

I'm sure we'll meet again.

Family Portrait

Before he came to the Union Pacific,
Charles Francis Adams Jr.
dabbled in law, in letters, enlisted
in the Union Army, fought
in Gettysburg,
and rose to colonel at the end of the war.

This new position
he did not ask for, but they wanted him
to use his good name
to beg the Treasury for leniency
and save the company. But he has lost
his first fight
to that hoodlum from Denver, that cow town
in the great, fat, dreary West.

The portraits of his forefathers
look at him from lacquered oak walls—

> John Adams
> Second President of the United States

> John Quincy Adams
> Sixth President of the United States

> Charles Francis Adams
> State Senator, Foreign Minister

How can he leave a legacy
worthy of his family?

China Mary

September 1884
Evanston, Wyoming

The last time I saw him, he told me
he could no longer see me:

he had a wife and two boys waiting
for him at home, and he needed to save
all his money—

Yesterday he came over with a pipe
of opium, saying he needed
to talk to someone and I was the only

person he could trust—

"You mean I'm the only woman you know
in this lonesome place,"

I said, but he wasn't listening,
he just sat in a corner of my shack smoking
his pipe, his eyes

fixed on the wooden slats beneath the window.

We sat there in silence, passing
the pipe between us—

"Where did I go wrong? I came to America,
I worked hard, I built the railroad,
my back hurts,

I can't wash off the coal dust
from my hands and still I cannot go home!"

He kicked off his shoes.

"And now those white rascals have put a target
on our backs. We are the enemy."

He paced the room, puffing the pipe.

"I never got to say goodbye
to my mother. What if I never get to see
my wife and children again?"

He stayed the night for old time's sake, even
left me some money—

What I did not say is
at least he has a family waiting for him,
a home to haunt his dreams:

I have nowhere to go but this wasteland.

First Snow

September 1884
Denver, Colorado

Coal miners in Colorado asked
Joseph Buchanan to organize them.

There are two things you need for a
successful strike:

One, a just cause.

Two, a way to win.

You have a just cause,

but you don't yet have a path
to victory.

Go back to work.

It's not yet time to strike.

Let's wait till winter, when
they need us more.

On the first day I look out of my window
and see snow on the foothills,

I'll order the strike.

Winter Storm

October 1884
Louisville, Colorado

Winds slam down from the mountains so hard
that even the birds struggle to fly.

The sky is still clear, the air warm at dawn.

Autumn leaves, dried up and ready to drop,
whip into a steady rumble on the trees.

He grips his lunch pail and shields his face
as he walks right into a squall.

At the bathhouse, he shivers as he changes
into a light shirt and his boots.

Ten hours later, as he leaves the mine,
dark clouds begin to gather on the plains.

In the dusk light, he sees the peaks
blue in the distance are streaked with snow.

Ornament

December 1884
Omaha, Nebraska

Samuel Callaway replaces S. H. H. Clark
as the general manager of the Union Pacific.

Cedar embers fade in the hearth.

He shuffles the gifts
under the tree,

stuffs the stockings
with candy—

His hand trembles.

The glass slips from his grasp,
shattering the star.

IV. A Severe Struggle

Letter Home

January 1885
Rock Springs, Wyoming

I don't want to make you worry, but I don't know
who else I can tell. Last fall, the union
in Denver called for a strike in the mines. Here

in Rock Springs, they set fire to the machine shop
at Number One. In Carbon, the strikers
were all dismissed. Now they block the mines,

their guns square at their hips, threatening anyone
who would replace them. They're still out there
in the biting cold of winter, demanding

the company dismiss us. They call us
a foreign menace. They're full of themselves, but
maybe it's time to go home. Yet I can't stop thinking

of that year we didn't even have rice to eat.

On the Wire

January & February 1885
Omaha, Nebraska

To C. F. Adams Jr. Esq.

No settlement has been made
with the miners at Carbon.

They are most unreasonable
in their demands, will not allow
any man to work at the mines.

S. R. Callaway

*

Men at Carbon have gone to work
on company terms.

S. R. Callaway

*

The Colorado miners all went out today
and are trying to get the Carbon
and Rock Springs men to join them—

They now want to name the price
at which we are to sell coal in Denver.

They cannot do it with my consent.

S. R. Callaway

*

Colorado's mines still out,
they are doing everything possible to get
operating force to join them.

Such participants as the Omaha bedlam
are endeavoring to aid them
in making trouble.

S. R. Callaway

*

Mr. Callaway in Toronto telegraphs
this morning, sister still living but very low.

Weather favorable, reports
indicate trains moving regularly.

Colorado coal men have resumed work
unconditionally.

J. M. Orr

Railroad Man

March 1885
Omaha, Nebraska

After his father died, Samuel Callaway
went to work as a clerk

on the Grand Trunk Railway, the beginning
of his life as a railroad man.

He was thirteen. Now thirty-four,
he is the general manager

of the Union Pacific, in charge of
thousands of miles of road in the prairies

of the West. A wife and three children
too, the family he never had.

A safe man, the boss says.
An affectionate man, friends say.

Generous. Always does
the right thing.

Now the boss is saying he regrets
appointing a coward

to the job. The workers
threaten a revolt.

Strike after strike.
How much more can he give?

How much more can he take before
he loses everything again?

Wings

March 1885
Rock Springs, Wyoming

"No work today," the foreman says
and sends him home without pay. Not wanting
to face his wife, he walks

to the hills, where birds
are starting to return. There he watches

a train slither into town. He spits on the ground.

Chinamen pour out of boxcars
and march in line toward the mines. He hurls
his tools at a pile of rocks

and stomps in the muddy snow.
"As long as they're here, there's nothing for us!"

A baby bird cries. He finds it tangled
in sagebrush and cradles it
on the long scar in his left palm.

"Come here, little one. Where did Mother go?"

Heathens

April 1885
Rock Springs, Wyoming

They don't believe in God.

They worship demons, false idols.

Look at their joss house, always burning paper.

It stinks.

They have no sense of right and wrong.

They come here as coolies, no better than slaves.

They break the law.

The Exclusion Act is supposed to keep them out.

But they still come in hordes.

They cannot assimilate.

Chinatown is a den of vices.

Opium. Gambling.

And their women, all prostitutes.

They lure our good men and corrupt them.

They wreck our families.

The Chinese must go!

Dream Factory

May 1885
Rock Springs, Wyoming

Some nights she still hears the whistle that blew
when they carried Daddy's body
from the mine.

"Rock fall. We're sorry, but
there's nothing else that we can do."

A week later, her brother,
just past fifteen,
took their father's tools and shoes

and showed up for work at Number Five.

Every day she begs
the Lord to bring him home alive.

Every day she sees the gash on Daddy's scalp,
the eyes still open—and the hands,
those blistered hands

he can no longer lay on her.

China Mary

June 1885
Evanston, Wyoming

What if I did not take that boat
to America thirty years ago?

I did not see another way out—
my parents sold me, their only girl,
to an old man who had a wife
and two concubines. I scrubbed
the floors as the wife beat me
and at night I did whatever it took
to please the man. I ran back
to my mother and father but they
said they had spent my dowry
and made me return to the house.

The captain said I could cook
in exchange for board. And he left me
alone, unlike some of the girls
he summoned to his room
at night. But when we docked
in San Francisco, he took me
to an alley and sold me
to the highest bidder, a parlor
house at the heart of Chinatown.

I would rather not talk about
this time in San Francisco. After
two years a customer wanted
to marry me, paid off my debts
so I could leave the house
with all its jewels and silk behind

for a new life amid the dust
and silver of the Comstock Lode.

Now I live in this bleak town
alone, comforting the men so far
from home, but I never
have to scrub the floors. At first
I thought I would go crazy, talking
to the moon and stars to fill
the silence, but I no longer have
to answer to anyone. I know
the lines that I should not cross
and no one will bother me—

I watch the white men
drink in bars and talk about how
we Chinese ruin everything,
how much they want
to strike and kick us out—

I watch the white women
grab their children as they pass me
on the street, muttering
crude things they think I cannot
understand, oh sweet ladies—

But where else can I go?

I watch the moon rise
and a lone star flits across the sky.

Law and Order

July 1885
Boston, Massachusetts

S. R. Callaway:

It has come to my attention
that the company's use of troops

in 1875
may not have been legal.

Find out whether
in the event of an insurrection

we will be able
to call on the Army.

Respectfully,

C. F. Adams, Jr. Esq.

Down in the Shaft

July 1885
Rock Springs, Wyoming

The foreman bristles as he hears the laughter
from the next room, miners
talking loudly about the loose women

they meet at the saloon, the shocking things
they do under the cover of night,
and as he crosses himself

he looks at the pile of tailings no one
has bothered to remove, a health
and fire hazard, and he tells himself that if

these men were quiet and diligent
like the Chinese, focused
on getting the job done rather than finding

ways to slack off and leave early,
they would not have anything to complain
about, and the company

would not need to replace them
with those slant-eyed yellow men who eat
dogs and rats and who knows

what else they do in their hovels, he shudders
just to think about it, he wants
to wash this stubborn dust off his hands.

Deluge

August 1885
Rock Springs, Wyoming

Dark clouds gather over

the crags and cliffs, the fat

stalks of wheatgrass

on the verge of yellow

in the blinding heat. Winds

gust and women hold

their windows shut, praying

the glass will not rattle

and break. The sky rips

open and the streets

turn into rivers of mud

and twigs. Men dash into

the sheds and saloons,

their overalls dripping into

their boots. Lightning

splits a tree. A last burst

of hail before the sun

comes out again—

The Chinese Problem

August 28, 1885
Denver, Colorado

John Lewis of the Knights of Labor
          to Beckwith, Quinn & Company

It pains me greatly to have to call
to your attention the fact

that the Chinese problem at Rock Springs
is assuming a grave attitude.

Were it not for the fact that I am sensible
there will be an outburst

of indignation against these people,
I would not trouble you

with correspondence upon the matter.
But sensible as I am that

unless a change is effected immediately
there will be an outbreak,

I respectfully notify you of the storm
that is brewing.

It's useless for me to beat around the bush
in this matter.

The consequences are inevitable.

A Severe Struggle

August 28, 1885
Denver, Colorado

John Lewis of the Knights of Labor
to the Union Pacific Coal Department

Although I have been laying sick
for the past four weeks,

I have been flooded with correspondence
from Wyoming,

the sum and substance of which
is that the Chinese

are having all the work they can do
while our men at Rock Springs

are left out in the cold.
I understand they are now working

almost day and night,
while the Carbon men have worked

but one day in the last two weeks.
This makes the situation

terribly aggravating
and in spite of my efforts,

will undoubtedly result in a severe struggle
if longer continued.

For God's sake do what you can
to avoid this calamity.

The pressure is more than I can bear.

Letter Home

Things are getting worse here, dear.

There are posters all over town
asking us to leave or face
the consequences. In Rawlins

and Laramie they beat up Chinese
just for walking in the streets. The whites
have been threatening to strike

all summer long, but they cannot
as they have no work to do.
They're cowards. Their words are louder

than their actions. But the boys
are grown now. I never
saw them grow up. I want to go home.

We'll make it work, won't we?

V. The Chinese Must Go

Daybreak

September 2, 1885
Rock Springs, Wyoming

He wakes to blackbirds
rustling outside his window,

ready to fly away
for winter. His back aches

as he rolls out of bed, fumbles
for a light, boils water

for tea, chews on a slice
of dry bread—no more butter.

He grabs his tools and heads into
the hazy dawn. Dew droplets

nip his skin. Along the banks
of Bitter Creek, sagebrush

scrapes his shins. The sun
casts a long light on the land.

Chinatown Burning

September 2, 1885
Rock Springs, Wyoming

On the last day of August, like the end
of every month, foreman Jim Evans shuts
the mines and reassigns the rooms. He marks
two rooms for the Chinese at Number Six,
entry five, and tells Isaiah Whitehouse
and William Jenkins they can take the room
beyond theirs. In summer the white men mined
in entry seven, where the air was bad
and management refused to pay for digging
an airway. But at least the men had work.

Isaiah Whitehouse came to America
from England's coal country at twenty. Coal
is what he knows. He worked in Pennsylvania
before he came out West and learned to fight
for workers' rights. That spring he ran for a seat
in the legislature and easily won
Sweetwater County's vote. He speaks to men
who yearn for fellowship and dignity.

First of September, Whitehouse starts to work
in a room beyond the Chinamen, just as
Jim Evans said. For a few hours he chisels
away, dust in his eyes, and sets some charges
in the unyielding rock.

              That night the bells
in the union hall ring out across the hills.
It is not known what the white men discussed.

The morning of September 2nd, Whitehouse
and Jenkins reach the mine, only to find
that two Chinese are working in their room.
All that hard work. Those dirty rats have fired
the charges and are reaping the rewards of
the white men's work. It is most likely that
Jim Evans had marked off this very room
for the Chinese, but he was not exact
when he instructed the white men to take
"the room beyond theirs." Angry, the white men
tell the Chinese to leave and the Chinese
tell them the pit boss said this is their room.

It is not known who threw the first punch
but these four men begin to brawl with picks,
shovels, and tamping needles, trading blows
as other miners, both white and Chinese,
come to their aid. Whitehouse takes a tumble
when a pick strikes his belly. Three white men
wrestle the Chinaman and drive a pick
into his skull. The men beat up another
Chinaman, hit his head with a cracked shovel.
Foremen arrive and move the injured men
into pit cars. Jim Evans tries to talk
to the white men but they just brush him off.
"Come on, boys! We may as well finish it now,"
they smirk. "It has to be done anyhow."

All the white men storm off the job, go home
for their guns, clubs, and knives, and they begin
to march into town along the railroad tracks,
chanting, "White men fall in! White men fall in!"
They gather at the union hall and take
a vote: another meeting in the evening
at six. The Chinese problem must be settled.

The men disperse. With nothing else to do
they storm the bars, toss back too many pints,
carousing till the keepers kick them out
at noon and close the taverns. Now they mingle
in the streets, hurling coal at the Chinese
who happen to be walking by and shooting
imaginary birds above their heads.

"Stamp out the yellow plague!

                    The Chinese must go!"

The Chinese think the white men only know
to talk, not act, and pay them little heed.

At two o'clock, a rumor goes around:
the company has asked for troops to crush
this insurrection. The white men decide
they must take things into their own hands
and drive the Chinese out of this damn town.
"If we don't act now, boys, they'll put us down!"
A hundred, now a hundred fifty strong,
the mob begins to march toward the bridge
on Bitter Creek, stopping at the gun store
to buy up all the ammunition, shooting
the sky as they close in on the Chinese.
"Listen, John Chinamen! You have one hour,
one hour to leave town!" The mob stands guard
on the main bridge out of Chinatown.

Many Chinese can't tell if they should take
these white men seriously—the company
will send their guards to put the hoodlums down,
won't they? Many of them have not yet heard
about the fight at Number Six, the blood
shed deep inside the earth earlier this day,

but still they raise a lone red flag to warn
their countrymen of danger near their homes.
They can make out the mob as they return
from the mines, hills, and shops, the other side
of Bitter Creek, their bellies full of soup.

At three o'clock, another rumor spreads:
the Chinese are armed and ready to defend
their property. White men: it's time to act.

The mob splits up into three squads. The first
crosses the bridge that leads to Chinatown.
A second group seals off another bridge
on the south side of town. And the third gang
charges up the hill to Number Three,
shooting at the coal shed and the pump house.
Three Chinamen sought refuge in the shed
and bullets hit them as they try to flee.
Their bodies tumble into Bitter Creek.

Crowds gather on the streets to watch the mob.

The Chinese flee from Chinatown "like a herd
of hunted antelopes." Many of them
dash out onto the streets without their shoes,
wearing little more than their blue jackets,
gathering only the belongings they
can carry on their backs. A few have nothing
at all, not even coins, as they crawl down
the banks of Bitter Creek, their feet sliced up
by thorns. They trample through the muck and silt,
the dirty water stinging their fresh wounds,
and climb back up to reach the sagebrush hills
east of Burning Mountain. But they escaped.
Others are beaten, robbed, and shot, their bodies
strewn in the streets and bleeding in the dirt.

A young white woman towers on a bridge,
an infant on one hip, a pistol cocked
in her right hand. She aims at the Chinese
and hits the back of a man's head. The baby
wails at the crack of gunshots and she spanks
the child, lays the bundle on the ground,
lifts up her foot and stomps the man's head in.

"Stamp out the yellow plague!

                    The Chinese must go!"

By four o'clock, not one Chinese is seen
out on the streets alive. Either they've fled,
crawling like small blue dots on Burning Mountain,
or they are hiding in their cellars, waiting
for the white men to stop their rampage. For
a moment all is quiet in Rock Springs.

Edward Murray, town doctor, waves his hat
as he rides a horse through town, rousing the mob
and barking, "No quarter! Shoot them down!"
He tells the rioters they must set fire
to Chinatown—homes, shops, and all—so that
nothing is left for the Chinese if they
choose to return. The wooden houses crackle
and the smoke chokes the men who chose to hide
inside their cellars. Some of them rush out
coughing, their long pigtails alight, their hands
shielding their mouths and eyes. Others are trapped
beneath their homes, trying to find a way
to beat the flames and the rising, deadly heat.

Out in the hills, the Chinese watch the blaze
engulf what they once called—not so much home,
but a place where they have friends who shared the pain
of living in this strange country alone.

The flames lap at the stashes of gunpowder
the miners keep beside their tools. Explosions
rattle the streets and echo past the cliffs.

Across the creek, the crowd cheers on each blast.

Eleanor Thirloway arrived in town
less than a year before to join her father,
a man who preaches all that's good and holy.
She teaches English to the Chinamen,
her act of charity before the Lord,
and she regards herself as their good friend.
They huddle at her door and ask if she
would hide them in her cellar. Her head turned,
she says, "It is not safe for you to stay.
Right now it's better if you all leave town."

After the flames die down, she is seen sifting
for loot amid the ruins of Chinatown.
Later, she and her father would tell a jury
they saw—with their own eyes!—the Chinamen
set fire to their homes before they fled.
"They were afraid white men would find their money."

David Thomas, mine boss at Number Five,
is standing on a tipple when he hears
there was a fight at Number Six. He looks
across the hills and sees a fierce commotion
over at Number Three. He makes his way
to Chinatown and tells five or six friends
it looks like trouble's brewing—so be careful.
He came to town some seven years ago
as a driver in the mines and worked his way up
the company ranks. This is his home now.

On his way back to Number Five, the mob
stops at the railroad crossing and begins

to shoot at the Chinese. He turns around
and heads for home, fearful of the next thing
the mob might do. He sees a woman walk
to the dead body of a Chinaman
and take his packages of laundry. Next
he sees another laundryman escape
into his dugout and a group of thugs
climb up his roof to kill him. "We had to,
you know, he came at us wielding a knife."

He sees the body of a man he knows
slumped in the dirt and bleeding from a shot
to his bare chest. For a moment he considers
putting the man out of his misery,
but he could not do it. He sees hogs eat
some charred remains and for a long time after
he could not bring himself to feast on pork.

Later, when asked to serve on the grand jury,
he turns it down and tells the sheriff straight,
"I do not feel my back is bulletproof."

At six o'clock, some rioters go home
for dinner—who knows what their wives exclaim
when they show up covered in blood, their eyes
telling a story no one wants to hear.
And who knows what they tell their children as
they eat their sausages and cold potatoes.
At dusk, they finish what they started back
in Chinatown: they march through the dim streets
carrying torches, setting what is left
ablaze and tossing bodies in the flames.

A plume of thick smoke drifts into the sky.

Letter Home

September 3, 1885
Evanston, Wyoming

How do I begin to tell you what happened? The white devils came for us. They broke into our homes and shot at us. They blocked both bridges out of town. I scrambled across the creek and ran into the hills. Cacti stung my feet but I kept running. I saw smoke rising and knew it had to be from our part of town, but I didn't want to look back. I had only the clothes on my back. At night dew froze on the grass and I had nothing to eat. I found the tracks and followed them. A train came by. The conductor tossed me a blanket and said, get on. Dearest, I can't come home.

The Names of the Dead

As reported by Huang Sih Chuen,
Chinese consul to New York.

Bodies found mutilated.

Leo Sun Tsung, 51.
Bullet in left jaw, injured right knee.
Found in his hut.
Mother, wife, and son at home.

Leo Kow Boot, 24.
Bullet in windpipe, neck severed.
Found near the mines.
Family unknown.

Yii See Yen, 36.
Bullet in left temple, skull broken.
Found near the creek.
Mother at home.

Leo Dye Bah, 56.
Bullet in chest, broken breastbone.
Found by the bridge.
Wife, son, and daughter at home.

Choo Bah Quot, 23.
Bones scorched, flesh on back gone.
Found at camp.
Parents at home.

*

Parts of dead bodies
found in piles of ashes
in their huts.

Sia Bun Ning, 37.
Found head, neck, and shoulders.
Mother, wife, son, and daughter at home.

Leo Lung Hong, 45.
Found head, neck, and breast.
Wife and three sons at home.

Leo Chih Ming, 49.
Found head and chest.
Mother, wife, and son at home.
Another son in the mines.

Liang Tsun Bong, 42.
Found head, hands, and shoulders.
Wife and two sons at home.

Hsu Ah Cheong, 32.
Found skull bone, jawbones, and teeth.
Parents, wife, and son at home.

Lor Han Lung, 32.
Found sole and heel of left foot.
Mother, wife, son, and daughter at home.

Hoo Ah Nii, 43.
Found right half of head and backbone.
Wife at home.

Leo Tse Wing, 39.
Found bones from hip to foot.
Family unknown.

*

*Twelve fragments of bones
found in twelve different places
in Chinatown.*

*No traces found
of the remaining three persons.*

Leo Jew Foo, 35.
Mother at home.

Leo Tim Kwong, 31.
Family unknown.

Hung Qwan Chuen, 42.
Father at home.

Tom He Yew, 34.
Mother, wife, and daughter at home.

Mar Tse Choy.

Leo Lung Siang.

Yip Ah Marn.

Leo Lung Hon.

Leo Lung Hor.

Leo Ah Tsun.

Leang Ding.

Leo Hoy Yat.

Yuen Chin Sing.

Hsu Ah Tseng.

Chun Quan Sing.

Notes

There are "two kinds of reaching in poetry," writes Muriel Rukeyser, "one based on the document, the evidence itself; the other kind informed by the unverifiable fact, as in sex, dream, the parts of life in which we dive deep and sometimes—with strength of expression and skill and luck—reach that place where things are shared and we recognize the secrets."

The events I describe in this book are based on document and evidence, as elaborated below. In fictionalizing this story in verse, I also aim to inhabit the lived experience of this history. All the named characters are based on historical figures. With a few exceptions, the unnamed characters are my invention. Their stories are absent from the records, but I depend on known circumstances to imagine their lives.

*

Craig Storti's *Incident at Bitter Creek: The Story of the Rock Springs Chinese Massacre* (Ames: Iowa State University Press, 1991) is one of the few comprehensive accounts of the massacre. It is also problematic. Most notably, Storti claims that the Rock Springs Massacre and the Chinese Exclusion Act have "little to do with race prejudice or immigration policy. The issue, rather, was the status of the American workingman in the industrial era."

The question of whether the Rock Springs Massacre was planned or spontaneous remains unresolved. Though ultimately inconclusive, Dell Isham makes a good argument that it was organized in his book *Rock Springs Massacre 1885* (Fort Collins: privately printed, 1969, 1985).

Charles Adams dispatched Isaac Bromley to Rock Springs to investigate the massacre. Bromley's report is published as *The Chinese Massacre at Rock Springs, Wyoming Territory, September 2, 1885* (Boston: Franklin Press, 1886).

Richard White's *Railroaded: The Transcontinentals and the Making of Modern America* (New York: W. W. Norton & Company, 2011) is a darkly comedic history of mismanagement and corruption on the transcontinental railroads.

Gerald E. Rudolph's *The Chinese in Colorado, 1869–1911* (Master's Thesis, University of Denver, 1964) gives an overview of early Chinese immigration to Colorado and an account of the Hop Alley Riot.

In *The Story of a Labor Agitator* (New York: The Outlook Company, 1903), Joseph R. Buchanan tells of his early days as a labor organizer and his involvement in the strikes on the Union Pacific system in 1884 and 1885.

*

There are no known records of letters, journals, or other such primary documents written by the Chinese who built the transcontinental railroad or worked in the mining camps of the interior West.

In the early 1900s, Chinese people in San Francisco formed poetry clubs. Marlon K. Hom's *Songs of Gold Mountain: Cantonese Rhymes from San Francisco Chinatown* (Berkeley and Los Angeles: University of California Press, 1987) is an anthology and translation of their folk rhymes. These poems depict the fears, hopes, and joys of the Chinese who lived in the United States during the era of Chinese exclusion.

Gordon H. Chang's *Ghosts of Gold Mountain: The Epic Story of the Chinese Who Built the Transcontinental Railroad* (New York: Houghton Mifflin Harcourt, 2019) seeks to present a full account of the story of the Chinese who worked on the Central Pacific from a point of view that honors their agency and humanity.

Erika Lee's *The Making of Asian America* (New York: Simon & Schuster, 2015) is a comprehensive history of Asians in the Americas, from the Spanish colonization of Latin America through the industrialization of the American West to the global challenges of today.

*

China Mary is based on a real-life woman who died in Evanston, Wyoming, on January 13, 1939. She was one of the town's characters, charging tourists ten cents to take her picture, and told fanciful stories of her life.

The records of her life are scarce and inconsistent. She shows up in the Evanston census in 1910, 1920, and 1930, each time with a different year of immigration to the United States, and the ages recorded in the census do not match the age on her death certificate.

In some accounts, she lived in Evanston for at least sixty years before her death. She may have been a cook in Bear River City in 1868, where she witnessed a vigilante lynching in November of that year. She is believed to have worked as a prostitute at one time and eventually became the first Chinese woman to own property in Evanston.

There is also circumstantial evidence that she lived in Park City, Utah, before she arrived in Evanston. In some accounts, she owned a China ware shop with a husband in Park City in the 1880s. It is likely that she was in Park City, but the exact timeline is difficult to ascertain.

The 1880 Census identifies two Chinese brothels in Evanston. It also lists one Chinese woman in Rock Springs, the wife of a Chinese doctor.

*

I also used documents, correspondence, reports, newspaper articles, and other materials from the following archives:

Wyoming State Archives, Cheyenne, Wyoming: Sweetwater County Court Journal, Rock Springs Chinese Riot Clipping File.

American Heritage Center, University of Wyoming, Laramie, Wyoming: Francis E. Warren Papers; Clarice Whittenburg Papers; T.A. Larson Papers; Grace R. Hebard Papers; Report No. 2044 of the 49th Congress, "Providing Indemnity to Certain Chinese Subjects"; "Chinese Riot" by David G. Thomas, as told to his daughter Mrs. J.H. Goodnough.

Sweetwater County Historical Museum, Green River, Wyoming: Sheriff's Jail Record; Criminal Dockets in Justice's Court, Rock Springs Precinct; Special File on Chinese Riot at Rock Springs, Wyoming, which includes the "Special Report of the Governor of Wyoming to the Secretary of the Interior concerning Chinese Labor Troubles, 1885."

Nebraska State Historical Society, Lincoln, Nebraska: Union Pacific Archives, in particular the Office of the President—Labor Disputes and the Annual Reports.

Denver Public Library, Denver, Colorado: *Rocky Mountain News* archives.

*

"The Names of the Dead" itemizes a report by Huang Sih Chuen, Chinese consul to New York in 1885. It does not include the names of those who might have perished in the hills.

These poems are composed entirely from found text: "Ultimatum," "Headlines," "Chinese Exclusion Act," "On the Wire," "Law and Order," "The Chinese Problem," and "A Severe Struggle."

Acknowledgments

This book would not have been possible without the steadfast work of archivists to preserve the (incomplete) evidence and ephemera of the past. I would like to thank the staff of the Wyoming State Archives, American Heritage Center, Rock Springs Historical Museum, Sweetwater County Historical Museum, Uinta County Museum, Nebraska State Historical Society, and Denver Public Library Special Collections for their insight, assistance, and patience at the photocopier.

Julie Kane, Tyson Hausdoerffer, Maya Jewell Zeller, David Rothman, and Ernest Hilbert—thanks for your guidance and mentorship as I tackled the challenges of this project and pushed the possibilities of my poetics. Kittens are the ideal subject for practicing metrical forms.

Gratitude to the editors of these journals, where some of these poems first appeared:

About Place Journal: "Wings" (Volume VIII, Issue I, May 2024).

Beloit Poetry Journal: "Chinese Camp," "Housekeeping" (Volume 72, No. 1, Spring/Summer 2022).

Diode Poetry Journal: "Faraway Places," "Expectant" (Volume 16, No. 1, March 2023).

The Georgia Review: "Chinatown Burning" (Summer 2022).

High Country News: "Letter Home, December 1873," "Letter Home, December 1875," "Letter Home, May 1882," "Letter Home, January 1885" (with introduction) as part of "The Rock Springs Riot Revisited," a text-image collaboration with Niki Chan Wylie (Volume 55, No. 9, September 2023).

South Dakota Review: "Number One," "Landlocked," "Iron Horse" (Volume 58, No. 1. Winter 2024).

Quarterly West: "Winter Storm," "Dream Factory," "Daybreak" (Issue 110, November 2023).

The magnificent team at Torrey House Press, Kirsten Johanna Allen, Will Neville-Rehbehn, Kathleen Metcalf, Gray Buck-Cockayne, Scout Invie, and Alexis Powell—thanks for inviting me into the fold, fostering dialogue on the difficult legacies of the American West, and shepherding this book into the world.

Every book is a journey that begins in failure and reaches an approximation of acceptance. Thanks to friends and family who held space for these tribulations.

About the Author

Teow Lim Goh is a poet and essayist who writes from the nexus of people and place. One of her ongoing projects is to recover the histories of Chinese immigrants in the American West. She is the author of two previous poetry collections, *Islanders* (2016) and *Faraway Places* (2021), and her essay collection *Western Journeys* (2022) was a finalist for the 2023 Colorado Book Awards in Creative Nonfiction.

About the Cover Art

Bloomer Cut
2007, Chinese ink on paper,
8.75" x 12"

A small band of Chinese railway workers made the Bloomer Cut by using iron picks, shovels, and black powder. It was the first major task performed by Chinese workers in the construction of the Central Pacific Railway. At the time of its completion in 1864, it was considered the 8th wonder of the world.
Zhi Lin, Auburn, CA. January 2007

Torrey House Press

Torrey House Press publishes books at the intersection of the literary arts and environmental advocacy. THP authors explore the diversity of human experiences and relationships with place. THP books create conversations about issues that concern the American West, landscape, literature, and the future of our ever-changing planet, inspiring action toward a more just world.

We believe that lively, contemporary literature is at the cutting edge of social change. We seek to inform, expand, and reshape the dialogue on environmental justice and stewardship for the natural world by elevating literary excellence from diverse voices.

Visit www.torreyhouse.org for reading group discussion guides, author interviews, and more.

As a 501(c)(3) nonprofit publisher, our work is made possible by generous donations from readers like you.

Torrey House Press is supported by Back of Beyond Books, Bright Side Bookshop, The King's English Bookshop, Maria's Bookshop, the Jeffrey S. & Helen H. Cardon Foundation, the Lawrence T. Dee Janet T. Dee Foundation, the Stewart Family Foundation, the Barker Foundation, Robert Aagard & Camille Bailey Aagard, Kif Augustine Adams & Stirling Adams, James Allen, Diana Allison, Richard Baker, Patti Baynham & Owen Baynham, Klaus Bielefeldt, Joe Breddan, Karen Buchi & Kenneth Buchi, Rose Chilcoat & Mark Franklin, Linc Cornell & Lois Cornell, Susan Cushman & Charlie Quimby, Lynn de Freitas & Patrick de Freitas, Pert Eilers, Betsy Gaines Quammen & David Quammen, Laurie Hilyer, Phyllis Hockett, Kirtly Parker Jones, Rick Klass, Jen Lawton & John Thomas, Susan Markley, Leigh Meigs & Stephen Meigs, Kathleen Metcalf, Donaree Neville & Douglas Neville, Laura Paskus, Katie Pearce, Marion S. Robinson, Molly Swonger, Shelby Tisdale, the Utah Division of Arts & Museums, Utah Humanities, the National Endowment for the Humanities, the National Endowment for the Arts, the Salt Lake City Arts Council, and Salt Lake County Zoo, Arts & Parks. Our thanks to individual donors, members, and the Torrey House Press board of directors for their valued support.

Join the Torrey House Press family and give today at
www.torreyhouse.org/give.

www.ingramcontent.com/pod-product-compliance
Lightning Source LLC
Jackson TN
JSHW071756020425
81876JS00009B/22